FINDING CHRIST
IN THE
OLD TESTAMENT
A STUDY

BIBLE STUDIES TO IMPACT THE LIVES
OF ORDINARY PEOPLE

Christian Focus Publications
The Word Worldwide

Written by Dorothy Russell

PREFACE

Where there's LIFE there's GROWTH:
Where there's GROWTH there's LIFE.

WHY GROW a study group?

Because as we study the Bible and share together we can

- learn to combat loneliness, depression, staleness, frustration, and other problems
- get to understand and love each other
- become responsive to the Holy Spirit's dealing and obedient to God's Word

and that's GROWTH.

How do you GROW a study group?

- Just start by asking a friend to join you and then aim at expanding your group.
- Study the set portions daily (they are brief and easy: no catches).
- Meet once a week to discuss what you find.
- Befriend others, both Christians and non Christians, and work away together

see how it GROWS!

WHEN you GROW ...

This will happen at school, at home, at work, at play, in your youth group, your student fellowship, women's meetings, mid-week meetings, churches and communities,

you'll be REACHING THROUGH TEACHING

INTRODUCTORY STUDY

OPEN MY EYES
What is the Bible?

a) a big, black, dull, uninteresting book?
b) 'the most valuable thing this world affords'?
c) an account of God's dealings with mankind?
d) an out-of-date piece of literature, no longer relevant today?
e) a book which the ordinary man needs explained to him by a theologian?
f) God's love-letter to man?
g) a book inspired by God, useful for teaching what is right and wrong, and helping us to do right?
h) essentially a revelation of God's nature, purpose, ways and deeds?

To the definitions above which you feel are correct, add this one: 'a book which speaks about Jesus Christ from beginning to end'. If this seems improbable to you, look up the following references:

Luke 24:27-32, 44-47.
John 5:39-40.
Acts 18:24-28.

* * *

Imagine you are a Jew living in Macedonia, Greece or Rome in the AD 50's. You know the beloved Old Testament Scriptures, which you read and study like any zealous person of your race; but you have not heard of a Galilean carpenter executed as a criminal some 20 years before. If you had heard of the event, you might not even have given it a passing thought.
Then, along comes Paul.
Read what happens   in Thessalonica   – Acts 17:1-4
                      in Berea   – Acts 17:10-12
                      and in Corinth   – Acts 18:1-6.

Discuss whether you would have been among those who believed or not, and why.
But for those who **did** believe, what Good News it was! The riddle of the Old

Testament Scriptures was being solved before their very eyes! The truths hidden there were at last being revealed. The mystery the prophets wrote about was unfolded to them (leaders, please see note on 'mystery' on page 42).

See how excited Paul was when he wrote to the people in Rome: Romans 1:2-4; 16:25-27.

If this 'mystery' which has been kept hidden for long ages past is to be revealed to us, we shall need to pray that God will OPEN OUR EYES as we do this study. So, we have a theme song. Learn it if you do not already know it, and sing it every time you meet!

1. Open my eyes that I may see
Glimpses of truth Thou hast for me;
Place in my hands the wonderful key
That shall unclasp and set me free.

Chorus
Silently now I wait for Thee,
Ready my God, Thy will to see
Open my eyes, illumine me,
Spirit Divine!

2. Open my ears that I may hear
Voices of truth Thou sendest clear;
And while the wave-notes fall on my ear;
Everything false will disappear.

3. Open my mouth and let me hear
Tidings of mercy everywhere;
Open my heart and let me prepare
Love with Thy children thus to share.

4. Open my mind that I may read
More of Thy love in word and deed;
What shall I fear while yet Thou dost lead?
Only for light from Thee I plead.

Used by permission

The book which has been very useful in the preparation of these studies is called *Christ In All The Scriptures*, by A. M. Hodgkin, (published by Christian Focus). This book has stood the test of time, having had 12 reprints, and having been translated into French, German, Italian, Arabic, Chinese and Japanese.

The opening paragraph of the Preface is too good to miss, and gives a wonderful picture of what is in store for us, as we explore the Old Testament in search of Jesus.

'On the glorious resurrection morning, Mary went to seek Jesus. She sought Him in the tomb, but He stood beside her. She thought He was the gardener but one word, "Mary", revealed to her her Saviour.

'As we read some passage in the Old Testament, how often our eyes are holden, and we see only the earthly form: we see Aaron the priest or David the shepherd, or Solomon the king: but if like Mary, we are really seeking the Lord Jesus, He manifests Himself to us through the outward type, and we turn in glad surprise, and looking up, say, "Rabboni – my dear Master".'

STUDY 1
I AM.
THE PRE-EXISTENT CREATOR

QUESTIONS

DAY 1 *Genesis 1:1-5, 26-27; John 1:1-5,14.*
a) How do the verses in John's Gospel add to our understanding of what happened in 'the beginning'?
b) Why does the Bible use 'us' and 'our' (instead of 'me' and 'my') in verse 26?

DAY 2 *John 17:5; Philippians 2:5-7.*
a) What can we learn about the Lord Jesus here?
b) Pray to Him now, thanking Him for what He gave up for your sake.

DAY 3 *Colossians 1:15-17; Hebrews 1:1-3, 10-12.*
a) Meditate on the majesty and wonder of the thoughts expressed here.
b) Pick out 2 things said about Jesus and for which you can especially praise Him (perhaps things new to you).

DAY 4 *Genesis 16:7-14; 32:24-30; Judges 13:2-22.*
a) What term is used for the Heavenly Person who appeared to Hagar and Manoah?
b) What conclusion did they, and Jacob, come to after meeting this Person?

DAY 5 *Genesis 18:1-8, 16-22.*
a) What can we find out about the Lord when He appeared to Abraham?
b) Joshua 5:13–6:2. How do we know that Joshua recognised this Man as the Lord?

DAY 6 *Judges 2:1-5; 6:11-24.*
a) How is 'the angel of the LORD' identified with God in these two readings?
b) Why was Gideon so afraid when he had seen this Being?

QUESTIONS (contd.)

DAY 7 *John 1:14; Galatians 4:4-5; Hebrews 2:14.*
a) In what 3 ways do these 3 readings describe what happened when Jesus became man?
b) How was this different from His Old Testament appearances?

NOTES

In this study I see Jesus *as the Creator God who existed before time began.*

* * *

When we are first 'introduced' to God in Genesis Chapter I, we see Him as the all powerful Creator: He created the light, the heavens and the earth, the sea and the sky and everything in them. Then 'He' revealed Himself as more than one Person when He said, 'Let us make man in our image'.

In the first chapter of John's Gospel, we saw that in 'the beginning' the Word was the instrument of creative activity. Here, then, is our first glimpse of God the Son at work. What we discover about God the Father, we can also know about God the Son (and God the Holy Spirit).

Our wonderful God is one God, yet three Persons. Don't be surprised if you find this a hard nut to crack! It is difficult for our finite minds to understand this, but we can accept it and that's where faith comes in. In the same way we can accept creation, for Hebrews II:3 tells us: 'By faith we understand that the universe was formed at God's command'.

Jesus, when praying to His Father just before He was to die on the cross, made reference to 'the glory I had with you before the world began' (John 17:5). And Paul, inspired by the Holy Spirit, wrote that Jesus existed as God eternally before He became a man.

We are left in no doubt, therefore, that our Lord Jesus Christ, whom we at this present time can know personally and love, is the One who has existed from all eternity, even before the dawn of time.

* * *

Imagine you are taking part in a stage performance. You are to play the part of a Red Indian! The theatrical make-up artist gets busy, a suitable costume is prepared, you practise your lines – and the show goes on.

What do people in the audience see? They see a Red Indian, who looks and speaks like a Red Indian. They don't consciously see you, because you are showing yourself to them as a Red Indian. But when the show is over, what happens? Off comes the make-up, the clothes ... and you are yourself again! You never actually were a Red Indian – to become one, you would have to be born into a Red Indian family.

This is perhaps an illustration (though a rather poor one) of what Jesus did when He appeared in human form in the Old Testament. He sometimes showed Himself for a brief time with the appearance of a man, then disappeared (Gen. 18). This Being is called 'The angel of the LORD', and we know that He is God shown to man in visible form.

But when the Word (Jesus) became flesh and dwelt among us, He acquired true humanity through His mother Mary, and actually became a human being who was born, grew, lived and died, and rose again.

* * *

When you wake up tomorrow morning:
Start the day by praising your Creator – Father, Son and Holy Spirit, in these words:

O Lord our Lord,
Your greatness is seen in all the world,
Your praise reaches up to the heavens!   (Ps. 8:1)

Do this every morning you can remember.

STUDY 2
THE ONE WHO WILL COME TO DELIVER

QUESTIONS

DAY 1 *Exodus 3:1-6,13-15.*
a) What does 'the angel of the Lᴏʀᴅ' tell Moses about Himself?
b) Why did some Jews try to stone Jesus in John 8:54-59?

DAY 2 *Exodus 3:7-9; Matthew 1:21; 20:28.*
a) Why were the Israelites suffering? What did God say He would do?
b) How is this a picture of Jesus?

DAY 3 *Exodus 16:2-4, 13-16; John 6:31-35,48-51 (read John 6:25-58 if possible).*
a) What comparisons did Jesus make between Himself and the manna?
b) How can Jesus be the 'bread' of your life?

DAY 4 *Exodus 17:1-6; 1 Corinthians 10:1-4; John 7:37.*
a) Why is this water from the rock a good illustration of what Jesus does for us?
b) Why do you think more people today don't take advantage of what Jesus offers?

DAY 5 *Numbers 21:6-9; John 3:14-15.*
a) What had to be done with the bronze snake before the people could be healed?
b) What did the people have to do?
c) What did Jesus have to do so that we might have eternal life?
d) What must we do?

DAY 6 *Genesis 6:13-18; 7:5-10, 19-23.*
a) What saved the lives of Noah and his family ?
b) Luke 17:26-30; John 3:18. A Day of Judgment is coming for this world. What must we do to be saved?

DAY 7 *Luke 19:10; Hebrews 2:14-15.*
a) From what does Jesus save us, or set us free?
b) Discuss the remark made by the chief priests in Mark 15:31.

NOTES

In this study I see Jesus *as the One who came to save me.*

* * *

We are all familiar with the way Jesus used parables to illustrate a truth He wanted to convey. How well we can understand that God loves us and wants to forgive us when we read the parable of the lost son, whose father waited day after day for him to come home!

So, in the Old Testament, the Holy Spirit used actual historical happenings to teach what the coming Saviour would be like.

- Just as God promised to set His people free from slavery in Egypt, so the Saviour will set free those who are slaves because of their fear of death.
- Just as Noah and his family were kept safe from the impending judgment of God by taking refuge in the Ark, so today we can make sure that we will be kept safe from the Day of Judgment by being 'in Christ'.
- Collecting manna in the desert saved the Israelites from hunger, starvation and death itself. Just try going without food for a few days and see how you feel! Spiritually, we're completely dependent upon Jesus for life – we need to 'feed on Him' every day.
- Water is even more vital for staying alive. We can't last long without it. Imagine that scene where Moses was leading a mob of rebellious, thirsty people through the wilderness.

'Why did you bring us up out of Egypt to kill us with thirst?' they yelled at him. But God came to the rescue. And Moses struck the rock. Can't you see the picture? Water gushing out, people amazed, incredulous ... then pushing, laughing, and shouting for joy as they hold out their hands and splash the life-giving water into their mouths. What an illustration!

'Whoever drinks the water I give him will never thirst,' said Jesus. Have you tasted that pure, water of life? Does it thrill you? Does it satisfy you?

- And remember the bronze snake lifted up on a pole? One look at that snake would deliver a person from death by poison. If you had been there, suffering from snake bite, would you have looked at the one on the pole, trusting it would heal you? Or would you have been too busy applying a tourniquet, thinking that was a more sensible thing to do?

* * *

Have you ever had to go to your waste bin and look for something you had thrown away by mistake? It's not very pleasant, poking around amongst rotten cabbage leaves and smelly meat bones covered in custard! In fact we wouldn't do it unless the article we wanted to salvage was very precious or important to us.

The word 'salvage' is the precise meaning of the word used in the verse: 'For the Son of Man came to seek and *salvage* what was lost' (Luke 19:10).

You may not think you are lost, but you are outside God's back door, unless you have asked Him to come and pick you out of the filth of living for self.

Hebrews 7:24-25 reads: 'Jesus ... is able, now and always, to *save* those who come to God through him'.

An idea:
During the coming week, think of one wrong habit you wish to be free from. Then each day, consciously ask the Lord to *deliver* you from this, promising to obey what He tells you to do.

STUDY 3

THE LAMB OF GOD

QUESTIONS

DAY 1 *Genesis 22:1-18.*
a) What parallels can you find in this story to the sacrifice of Jesus on Calvary?
(To help you, look up: John 3:16; 8:29; 19:16-18; Rom. 8:32.)
b) But no one type can picture all of what Christ did for us. Where does this story stop short? How does the ram complete the picture?

DAY 2 *Exodus 12:1-14; 1 Peter 1:18-20.*
a) What kind of a lamb were the people to choose?
b) What would the blood of the lamb do for them?
c) How is the passover lamb (1 Cor. 5:7) a picture of Jesus?

DAY 3 *Leviticus 1:1-13; Hebrews 10:8-10.*
a) The burnt offering symbolises Christ offering Himself completely to God. What are we asked to do in Romans 12:1?
b) How would you explain Ephesians 5:2 to someone who asked you what it meant?

DAY 4 *Leviticus 4:22-31.*
a) For what reason was this animal to be sacrificed?
b) Isaiah 53:5-10; 1 John 2:2. Spend a few minutes thinking how costly it was for Jesus to bring us forgiveness.

DAY 5 *Leviticus 16:5-10, 20-22.*
a) What was Aaron to do with the goat which was 'for the LORD'?
b) What was he to do with the other one?
c) What are we told about Jesus in 1 Peter 2:24?

DAY 6 *Leviticus 17:11-12; Hebrews 9:12-14, 22; 1 John 1:7.*
a) What is the significance of the blood of the animal being shed?
b) What can only the blood of Jesus accomplish?

QUESTIONS (contd.)

DAY 7 *Revelation 5:6-14.*
a) How is the Lord Jesus pictured in the revelation given to John?
b) Why do you think He is pictured like this?

NOTES

In this study I see Jesus *as the Lamb Who died in my place, and took away my si*n.

* * *

Can you imagine the shock and bewilderment that people must have felt when they first heard John the Baptist say (John 1:19): 'Look! There is the Lamb of God ...' as he pointed to the man Jesus, the carpenter from Nazareth? Think about it for a minute. What pictures would have floated into their minds! What fragments from the Old Testament, which they knew so well!

- Young Isaac saying, 'Where is the lamb for the sacrifice?' and old Abraham replying, 'God Himself will provide one.'
- The killing of the Passover lamb, which died in the place of the eldest son of the household so long ago. The Passover ceremony with which they would be familiar when the children ask, 'What does this ritual mean?' And father tells them how the Lord passed over the houses of the Israelites, because the lamb had been their substitute.
- The burnt offering, where the animal was sacrificed whole, and where the smell was a fragrant offering to God.

And what else is John the Baptist saying?

'He takes away the sin of the world.'

'This is mind-boggling,' they must have thought. 'Isn't John getting rather mixed up? How could this be possible?'
They knew about:

- The animal which they were required to bring to the priest as an offering to take away sin. It would be killed and sacrificed, and the one who had sinned unintentionally would be forgiven.
- The scapegoat, which had all the evils, sins and rebellions of the people of Israel confessed over it, and which symbolically took these things upon itself. It was then driven off into the desert, carrying their sins far away.
- The blood of the sacrifice, which was to be poured out on the altar, because blood, which is life, takes away people's sins.

How difficult it would have been for the people being baptised in the Jordan River that day to know what John was talking about. But his prophetic words were inspired, and as we dip into the Old Testament and read about the sacrifices, the shedding of blood, and God's way of forgiving man's sin, we can see clearly the foreshadowing of the Lord Jesus, the Lamb of God.

It was as if God said,

'Follow these rules for sacrifice in the meantime. Each of you can personally bring an animal to the priest. Confess your sin, and clearly understand the principle of that animal taking the punishment that you deserve. You can see it being killed, and know that it dies in your place. You, then, go free.'

But this was only a picture of the real thing. It was only a temporary means of having sins covered, which could be used until the one and only Lamb of God came to earth. He then gave His own life as a sacrifice to take away completely the sin of those who trust Him.

That Divine Lamb died in your place.

* * *

How can you make a 'sacrifice' to remind you of what Jesus has done for you?

Here is a suggestion:
This coming week, deny yourself something you would normally do (e.g. having a meal, watching a favourite TV programme, reading a magazine) and use the time instead to read and think about some part of God's Word, and to talk to Him about it.

STUDY 4
THE TABERNACLE (IMMANUEL – GOD WITH US) .

QUESTIONS

DAY 1 *Exodus 38:9-16; Revelation 7:13-15.*
a) Of what material was the enclosure to be made? (Note that this was white, symbolising perfection.)
b) Why does one usually erect a fence around something? What can you learn from this about the enclosure round the Tabernacle?

DAY 2 *Exodus 38:18; John 10:7-9.*
a) Write down the 4 colours used in the curtain over the entrance. What does each colour make you think of?
b) Of what use is a gate (or door)? Why did Jesus He was one?

DAY 3 *Exodus 38:1-7; Leviticus 1:1-9.*
a) In what way do you think the bronze altar reminds us of Christ?
b) Exodus 30:17-21; 38:8; Psalm 24:3-4. What was used to make the large bronze basin? Of what was the washing ritual a sign?

DAY 4 *Exodus 25:23-40; 30:1-8; 40:22-27.*
a) What 3 pieces of furniture were placed in the main part of the tent (called the 'Holy Place')?
b) How can the purpose of these 3 items be linked with the purpose for which Jesus came into the world? (Try to work this out before looking up John 6:35; 8:12 and Heb. 7:25 with Rev. 8:3).

DAY 5 *Genesis 3:23-24; Exodus 26:31-33.*
a) By comparing these 2 readings, discover what was the significance of the embroidered 'cherubim' or 'winged creatures' (GNB) on the inner curtain?
b) Matthew 27:45-51; Hebrews 10:19-20. What happened to the curtain when Jesus died? What significance has this for us?

QUESTIONS (contd.)

DAY 6 *Exodus 16:31-34; 25:10-16; Hebrews 9:4.*
a) What did the Ark (box, or chest) of the Covenant contain?
b) Compare these 3 items with the following verses, and discover how each one speaks of Jesus: John 6:31-35; Hebrews 4:14; 5:4-5;1 Peter 2:22.

DAY 7 *Exodus 25:17-22; Hebrews 4:16.*
a) Remembering that the winged creatures pointed to God's holiness, and that the box contained the Law, which no man keeps perfectly, what does the gold lid ('atonement cover' or 'mercy seat') in between the two, demonstrate (Heb. 9:5)?
b) What was this to do with the Lord Jesus (Rom. 3:24-26)?

NOTES

In this study I see Jesus *living amongst men, living with me.*

* * *

God planned to live among men in the tent known as the Tabernacle. Because of this, it had to be made exactly according to His instructions. We have seen how each detail was significant, and was a picture of the only way sinful man could come near a holy God. Through the Tabernacle, God taught His people that He was holy, perfect, and unapproachable except by those who would fulfil His requirements. He required the shedding of blood, and the offering of a sacrifice so that sins could be forgiven.

How marvellous it is to open our eyes and see that the whole sacrificial system of the Old Testament was just a preview of the real thing – Christ's sacrifice on the Cross to deal with sin once and for all.

God came to live among men in the person of His Son, Jesus. Colossians 2:9 says, 'For in Christ there is all of God in a human body' (LB). John 1:14 can be literally translated, 'The Word (Jesus) became flesh and tabernacled among us.' That is, He came and pitched His tent here for a while!

Once again, the plan God had prepared was followed in exact detail. Jesus said that He had come not to do His own will, but the will of Him who had sent Him. In Jesus, God showed people His standard of perfection and their inability to reach this standard. And He provided the Way – the one and only Way – for sinful man to come to Him; that 'one, true, pure, immortal sacrifice' on the Cross.

God still lives among His people. By means of the Holy Spirit, who lives within each one who belongs to Jesus, God is again in the midst of His people. Because of this, our bodies are the temples, or tabernacles, where God the Holy Spirit lives. What a staggering thought this is!

God will make His eternal home among His people. When the heaven and the earth we know have disappeared, and the Holy City, the new Jerusalem, comes down out of heaven from God, then God's home will be with men for ever. There will be no more death, no more grief or crying or pain. The old things will have passed away. Doesn't this thrill you? And can't you see how everything in God's plan for the Tabernacle was pointing forward to our Lord Jesus, so that this union of God and man would be possible?

* * *

A Challenge:

Try this and see how long you can keep it up. Every time you begin doing something, say to yourself, 'Jesus lives in me. He is doing this with me'. Compare notes next week.

STUDY 5
PROPHET AND PRIEST

QUESTIONS

DAY 1 *Exodus 19:1-7; Numbers 12:4-8.*
a) Why did God call Moses to the top of the mountain?
b) How did God treat Moses differently from other prophets?

DAY 2 *Deuteronomy 18:14-20; Acts 3:22-24.*
a) What was the description of the great prophet God promised to send?
b) How did Jesus identify Himself as a prophet in John 12:49-50?

DAY 3 *Isaiah 6:1-9; Jeremiah 1:4-9; Ezekiel 1:1-3; 2:6–3:4.*
a) In what ways were Isaiah, Jeremiah and Ezekiel commissioned to be prophets?
b) What do these 3 stories have in common? What significance does this have for us?
(Note also the interesting reference John made to Isaiah's vision in John 12:41).

DAY 4 *Luke 4:22, 32, 36.*
a) What amazed the people when Jesus began His ministry?
b) The minor (shorter) prophets in the Old Testament are the 12 books from Hosea to Malachi in your Bible. Look up chapter 1:1 in each of them and see what they generally say!

DAY 5 *Exodus 28:1-2; Leviticus 9:7; Hebrews 5:1-3.*
a) What was the function of the priests in Old Testament times?
b) Genesis 28:10-12; John 1:51. What can we discover about Jesus from these verses?

DAY 6 *Exodus 32:30-32; Esther 4:7-16.*
a) What have Moses and Esther in common here?
b) What can you find out about Jesus from Hebrews 7:21-27?

DAY 7 *Job 9:30-35; 1 Timothy 2:3-6.*
a) What was Job's problem?
b) How was the answer to it wonderfully provided in Jesus?

NOTES

In this study I see Jesus *as the One who brings God's message to me,* and *the One who takes my prayers and worship to God.*

* * *

Away back in history, God looked upon the nation whom He had chosen for Himself, but who had turned their backs on Him, and He longed to communicate with them. He wanted to tell them, "Here are My laws. If you obey them, I will be your God and you will be My people." So He chose Moses to bring this message to them.

This, then, was the work of a PROPHET. When we look at Moses doing this work, we can see ahead to the great Prophet who was to come and be God's supreme Communicator. So, looking at each prophet in turn, we catch a glimpse of our Lord bringing God's message to men.

* * *

Look back to Study 3. What was it about?

We saw there, how the lamb that was killed to take away sin was a picture of our Lord Jesus. But this sacrifice could not be brought direct to God by the man-in-the-street. He had to bring it to the priest, who was the intermediary.

In this week's study we see Jesus not only as the sacrifice, but also as the Priest who offers the sacrifice on our behalf. It is true (as we saw last week) that Jesus has made direct access to God the Father possible, but only to those who first give their lives to Him.

The Living Bible paraphrases I Timothy 2:5-6(a) beautifully: 'God is on one side and all the people on the other side, and Christ Jesus, himself man, is between them to bring them together, by giving his life for all mankind.'

Job's wistful longing for a go-between who could bear his needs to God Almighty, makes us want to cry – 'But Job, there *is* Someone who will not only plead your cause, but who died to rid you of that guilt complex! You are right in saying no soap can wash away your sin, but the blood of Jesus can cleanse you from all the filth you speak of."

And how glorious is that verse in Hebrews 7 which says: 'And so he is able, now and always, to save those who come to God through him, because he lives for ever to plead with God for them' (Heb. 7:25, GNB).

The prophets and the priests of the Old Testament showed clearly the work that would be accomplished by the death and resurrection of the Lord Jesus. Their work was simply in the physical sense, so that people could see, and do, and learn. The whole priestly system was a massive Visual Aid, used to teach spiritual truth. Jesus brought reality. He *was* God's message, the Word of God, and He is the living communication line between us and God.

> Let us then approach the throne of grace with confidence, so that we may receive mercy, and find grace to help us in our time of need (Heb. 4:16).

A Thought:
As you pray each day this coming week, remember that the Lord Jesus is waiting to carry your prayers to the throne of grace. Thank Him that it is possible for you to approach a Holy God through Him.

STUDY 6

GOD'S ANOINTED SON

QUESTIONS

The words 'Chosen One' or 'Anointed One' in our Bibles have the same meaning as 'Messiah' and 'Christ'. Look out for these words as you do this week's study.

DAY 1 *Psalm 2:1-6; Acts 4:23-28.*
a) Look up different versions to see how reference to God's Anointed (Chosen) One is translated in Psalm 2:2.
b) What is the attitude of earthly rulers to Him?
c) Who fulfilled this prophecy in Jesus' day?

DAY 2 *Psalm 2:7-9; 89:20-29.*
a) What things said about David in these verses also apply to the Messiah?
b) How will His greatness be shown to the world?

DAY 3 *Psalm 45:1-7; 101:1-4.*
a) For whom was Psalm 45 originally written?
b) What can we infer about this Psalm from Hebrews 1:8-9?
c) What does Psalm 101 tell us about the coming Messiah?

DAY 4 *Isaiah 59:17-20; 61:1-3, 10. (Do not use the Good News Bible for today's readings.)*
a) What is signified by the garments and armour that the Anointed One puts on?
b) How do these qualities enrich the meaning of His title in Isaiah 59:20?

DAY 5 *Psalm 72:8-14; Isaiah 9:6-7; 11:2-5.*
a) From the verses in Psalm 72, pick out what you think is the most important thing said about the king.
b) Read the Isaiah passages again, and think over how beautifully they apply to Jesus, the Christ.

QUESTIONS (contd.)

DAY 6 *Luke 2:8-14; John 4:25-29; 7:25-31,40-44.*
a) What reasons can you find in these verses for identifying Jesus with the long-awaited Messiah?
b) What caused some people to doubt this?

DAY 7 *Mark 8:27-33; 14:61-64.*
a) What did Peter discover about Jesus?
b) What was the High Priest's attitude to this truth?
c) What title did Jesus use when speaking of Himself, in both cases?

NOTES

In this study I see Jesus *as God's 'Chosen One' or 'Messiah'.*

* * *

The picture of the coming 'Anointed One' is built up by psalmist and prophet from the time of David onwards. Four characteristics of this Person shine out from the picture, and it was these that godly Jews were looking for in their expectation of the Messiah.

1. He would be a man chosen and appointed by God.
2. He would have dominion over the nations, and bring judgment on Israel's foes.
3. He would love justice, and set God's people free from oppression.
4. God would be active, and glorified in all that He did.

By New Testament times, the popular national hope was of a king like David, who would bring political liberation and conquest. As we have been reading the prophecies in this study, we have clearly seen Jesus. But to those who were waiting for the Lord's Anointed One to sweep down and overthrow the Roman army of occupation, Jesus didn't fit the picture at all. True, some of the miraculous things He did caused people to wonder, but most Jews had built up in their minds a picture of what the Messiah would be like, and could not see Jesus in that role.

In our reading for Day 7 you may have wondered why Jesus told Peter not to spread the word around that He was the Messiah. This seems to indicate that the word 'Messiah' meant to the Jews, something quite different from the true meaning, and Jesus did not want to be associated with the wrong concept. He was quick to use the term 'Son of Man' for Himself in reply, even though He did, in fact acknowledge that He was God's 'Chosen One'. Only to the Samaritan woman at the well (John 4:25-26) did He introduce Himself as the Messiah, because to her the title would convey the idea of a prophet like Moses, not a Jewish king.

Was this misconception of the role of Messiah, then, the reason why the Jewish nation did not accept Jesus and believe in Him?

It was a stumbling block to some, certainly, but there were other reasons. The New Testament makes it quite clear that people of His day rejected Him, not because they were Jews, but because they were normal men and women. Materialism, threat to power, unwillingness to submit, were all reasons for unbelief, as they are today in any society.

Remember, too, that the early Church in Jerusalem, with 3,000 converts increasing daily to 5,000, and continuing to grow and including a great number of priests – were all Jews! So perhaps we can see that, as the apostles used these and other passages to prove that Jesus was their long-awaited Messiah, the Jews, in fact, should have had more reason to believe than anyone else. (Paul also gives another reason for Jewish spiritual blindness in Rom. 11:25. See also Acts 18:5-6.)

Look at the first paragraph of these notes again.

An interesting study can be made of Isaiah 45:1-8, 13, where Cyrus, a heathen king, is 'chosen' (anointed) by God to be given power and authority to set God's people free to return to Jerusalem. It is clear that God is working through him for His own glory. The four characteristics of the Messiah can be found in the above verses. The difference with this 'anointed one' is that he does not know God.

* * *

Do you remember the prophecy about the Messiah in Isaiah 61 (Day 4)? Jesus applied it to Himself when He read from that passage: 'The *Spirit* of the Lord is on me, because he has *anointed* me to preach good news to the poor ...'

Peter tell us: 'God *anointed* Jesus of Nazareth with the *Holy Spirit* and with power.'

Paul adds: 'He (God) *anointed* us, set his seal of ownership on us, and put his Spirit in our hearts' (2 Cor. 1:21-22).

This, then, is our high calling as Christians. We have been anointed with the Holy Spirit to do God's work. Isn't that a tremendous thought?

THINK – of someone who is 'needy' (Ps. 72:12), and be like Jesus, help him or her in some way this week.

STUDY 7
THE SUFFERING SERVANT

QUESTIONS

DAY 1 *Isaiah 42:1-9.*
a) What characteristics were to mark the chosen Servant of God?
b) Matthew 12:14-21. How did Jesus fill this role? Can you think of any particular incidences when He fulfilled this prophecy?

DAY 2 *Psalm 40:7-8; Isaiah 49:1-10.*
a) Who did God also say was His servant?
b) What work was the Servant to be given?
c) Read Luke 4:16-21 and comment on these verses.

DAY 3 *Isaiah 50:4-10; 52:13-15; 53:1-3.*
a) What glimpses of Jesus can you see here?
b) What kind of reaction to His Servant did God foretell?

DAY 4 *Isaiah 53:4-12; Acts 8:30-35.*
a) What do you think Philip would actually have said to the official from Ethiopia, when he 'told him the good news about Jesus'?
b) C. T. Studd's motto was: 'If Jesus Christ be God and died for me, then no sacrifice can be too great for me to make for Him.' Discuss whether you think this is realistic for yourself or not.

DAY 5 *Psalm 22:1-18; Matthew 27:35-46.*
a) Pick out the verses in Psalm 22 which give an exact picture of what Jesus suffered on the cross.
b) How could you use Psalm 22:1 to help someone who felt forsaken by God?

DAY 6 *Psalm 31:5; 34:20; 41:9; 69:19-21.*
Here are four more pictures of what was going to happen to Jesus. What does each one tell us?
(If you need the New Testament references, they are: Luke 22:21; 23:36, 46; John 19:36.)

QUESTIONS (contd.)

DAY 7 a) What have you found in this week's study to show that God's Suffering Servant was not to be a Superman, but was to have a human nature.

b) Read Isaiah 53:4-10 again, and thank Jesus that He was willing to suffer that agony of body and spirit, to make it possible for you to be forgiven.

NOTES

In this study I see Jesus *as the obedient Servant of God, who suffered for me.*

* * *

Try to imagine the boy Jesus growing up in the home at Nazareth. He would be taught the Scriptures of the Old Testament, and we can imagine His boyish enthusiasm as He studied and learned. By the time He was 12 years old, He apparently knew that, in a unique way, God was His Father and He was the Son of God.

Just when did the awareness come to Him of His role as the Suffering Servant? We can't tell, but we can be sure He meditated a great deal on these very passages we have been reading.

Then came the time when He emerged into public ministry. As He went down into the water to be baptised by John, the heavens opened, and He heard the voice of His Father acknowledging Him, not only as His Son, but as the Servant with whom He was pleased (Isa. 42:1; Matt. 3:17).

Was this a moment of revelation of something which had previously been hidden from Him? Again, we don't know – but we do know that He was subsequently tempted by the devil to reject the Father's plan of suffering for Him, and instead, to win the kingdoms of the world to Himself by using His divine powers (Matt. 4:5-9). But He knew His Scriptures so well that He overcame this temptation. Just imagine the courage needed to go through with His Father's plan, even though He could see Himself mirrored in passages like Psalm 22 and Isaiah 53.

What is your Heavenly Father's plan for you? Do you ask Him, day by day? Are you, like the Divine Servant we see in Isaiah 50:4 (GNB), 'Every morning he makes me eager to hear what he is going to teach me'? Only in this way can we be sure we don't miss out on what He has planned for us.

You may find you have to endure physical suffering, as the Chosen Servant had to; you may experience the bitterness of friends turning against you; you may even be despised and rejected; BUT – *you will never be forsaken by God if you belong to Him.* Never. Because His Son and Servant Jesus was willing to take your place, and be forsaken instead of you. 'And now he can help those who are tempted, because he himself was tempted and suffered' (Heb. 2:18, GNB).

A Suggestion:
This week, visit someone who is suffering physically, mentally, or emotionally, and share something about this study with them.

STUDY 8
GOD'S PREPARATION

QUESTIONS

Pretend that you are living before the days of the New Testament. What can you find out about the One whom God would send to save His people, from these references?

DAY 1 a) *Genesis 3:14-15.*
b) *Genesis 12:3; 18:18.*
c) *Genesis 49:10; Isaiah 40:9.*
d) *Numbers 24:15-17.*

DAY 2 a) *Isaiah 7:14.*
b) *Isaiah 9:1-2.*
c) *Isaiah 11:1.*
d) *Micah 5:2.*

DAY 3 a) *Isaiah 60:3.*
b) *Hosea 11:1.*
c) *Isaiah 40:3-5.*
d) *Malachi 3:1.*

DAY 4 a) *Psalm 69:9.*
b) *Isaiah 40:11.*
c) *Isaiah 42:2.*
d) *Zechariah 9:9.*

Now look up the following verses, and match them with the ones above (i.e. write the appropriate reference beside the Old Testament one).

DAY 5 *Matthew 1:6-17.*
Matthew 2:1-2 and Revelation 22:16.
Matthew 2:9-11.
Matthew 2:13-15.
Matthew 11:7-10.

QUESTIONS (contd.)

DAY 6 *Mark 1:1-4.*
Luke 1:26-35.
Luke 2:1-6.
Luke 5:15-16.
Galatians 3:7-9,
I John 3:8.

DAY 7 *John 2:13-17.*
John 7:40-43.
John 10:11.
John 12:12-15.
Hebrews 7:13-14.

NOTES

The readings in them are like the pieces of a jigsaw puzzle. When we put them together, we see Jesus.

* * *

Think of some big event where you might be involved in the preparation. It might be a wedding, an evangelistic Crusade, a stage performance, or simply Christmas! So many different things must be done, and people must be notified or invited. The bigger the event the more people will have a share in the preparation.

God has to prepare the world for the coming of His Son in human form, to bear the punishment for our sins. So, He sent messages to all kinds of different people down through the ages, and through them to the people of their day, and gradually the whole picture of the future event was built up.

Then when the right time finally came,

GOD SENT HIS SON (Gal. 4:4)

* * *

Let's go back to the Flood.

After it was over, Noah's three sons left the Ark, settled down, and fathered the peoples of the world. Even today, all nations can be traced back to these three men. But even at that early stage, God eliminated the descendants of two of Noah's sons, and blessed the third, Shem (Gen. 9:26). Through Shem would come the promised Messiah.

And so, through the centuries, the prophecies concerning the Messiah narrowed down the possibilities of which family God's Son would be born into, and eliminated all the others.

From all the descendants of Shem, He chose Abraham.
From the two sons of Abraham, He chose Isaac.
From the two sons of Isaac, He chose Jacob (Israel).
From the 12 sons of Jacob, He chose Judah.
From the descendants of Judah, He chose Jesse.
From the seven sons of Jesse, He chose David, and so on.

* * *

You may be familiar with the kind of puzzle which is solved by the process of elimination: e.g., Four men live in adjoining houses in Puzzle Street. Their names are Mr Red, Mr Blue, Mr Yellow and Mr Green. One of them has a son called

Jimmy, Jimmy's family live at No. 62. Mr Red's house is the only one without a '6' in its number. Jimmy lives next door to Mr Blue. The number of Mr Yellow's house is 2 more than Mr Green's, and 4 more than Mr Red's. Which man is Jimmy's Father? (You had better wait till you get home to figure this out!)

* * *

We stand amazed at the accuracy of the prophecies in the Old Testament considering that often the men who wrote them did not realise the full truth of their words. Yet is it so surprising, when we know that God inspired His Word? In those early days, God's people caught glimpses of HIS PLAN, and later, when Jesus came, they could look back and prove from these prophecies that Jesus was the promised Messiah.

Sometimes we read in the Gospels that Jesus did or said things to fulfill what the prophets had said (e.g. Matt. 4:14; 13:35).

Query:
How would you answer a person who said, 'It's not surprising that Jesus fulfilled prophecy, for He deliberately set out to do so'?

Discuss this as you close the study.

STUDY 9

RISEN, GLORIOUS LORD

QUESTIONS

DAY 1 *Psalm 16:10; Acts 2:22-33; 13:34-37.*
a) What event central to our faith, was anticipated in Psalm 16:10?
b) How did Peter and Paul show that David himself did not fulfil this prophecy?

DAY 2 *Isaiah 25:8; 1 Corinthians 15:54-57.*
a) Since people still die, how can Isaiah's words be true today?
b) Isaiah 53:10-12. How is Christ's resurrection implied here?

DAY 3 *Job 19:25-27; 1 Corinthians 15:20-23, 42-44; Philippians 3:20-21.*
a) Job was longing for a mediator between him and God (see *Study 5, Day 7*). How does his flash of inspiration in these verses help him? Do you have this assurance?
b) What promises are there for believers in these passages?

DAY 4 *Jonah 1:1-17; Matthew 12:38-41.*
Jonah is the only Old Testament prophet that Jesus directly compared Himself with. What similarities can you find? And what differences?

DAY 5 *Jeremiah 31:31-34; Luke 22:20.*
a) How would the new covenant foretold in Jeremiah, differ from the old one (Exod. 24:3-8)?
b) How were both covenants sealed?
c) Ephesians 1:19, 20. What was needed to make it possible for us to keep the new covenant?

DAY 6 *Hosea 3:5; Philippians 2:9-11.*
a) How is the Promised One described here by Hosea?
b) To what do these readings point?

DAY 7 *Daniel 7:13-14: Matthew 28:16-20: Revelation 11:15.*
a) Daniel saw Jesus in a vision. What was he shown about Him?
b) In what way can these verses help you to face the present world situation?

NOTES

In this study I see Jesus *breaking free from the bonds of death, alive for evermore!*

* * *

If we could assemble these men together –

> David
> Isaiah
> Job
> Jonah
> Jeremiah
> Hosea
> and Daniel

– what a formidable array of Old Testament 'greats' we would have!

Imagine these men being interviewed on a TV programme. The following questions are directed to them – see if you can remember the answers they would give.

DAVID, with regard to 'the world of the dead' (as you understood it), what did you foresee for God's faithful Servant?

ISAIAH, how did you show that suffering and death would not be the end for God's Chosen One?

JOB, how did you predict the resurrection of your Redeemer, and after Him, all believers?

JONAH, in your life, you unwittingly acted out what would happen in the future. Can you tell us about it?

JEREMIAH, looking into the future, you saw a Golden Age which was to come. How was it to be different from your own day?

HOSEA, you also saw a significant change ahead, centred around a descendant of David. What was it?

DANIEL, you had a vision of God's Holy One. What was He to be given?

* * *

Our study this week has been drawn from a period between 1000 BC and 165 BC

Throughout these years there were brilliant flashes of prophecy pointing to the greatest miracle of all time – the resurrection of Jesus. How marvellous it is that we can dip into the Old Testament and see the Risen Christ shining from its pages. Peter says, 'So we are even more confident of the message proclaimed by the prophets. You will do well to pay attention to it, because it is like a lamp shining in a dark place until the Day dawns and the light of the morning star shines in your hearts' (2 Pet. 1:19 GN).

The men who wrote these passages were not aware of the manner of fulfilment of their prophecies, nor of the fact that they foretold the supreme manifestation of God's mighty power. Has the enormity of it grabbed you yet? Have you realised that clever scholars have tried to disprove or explain away the Resurrection, only to be confronted with the undeniable truth of it? A lawyer, Frank Morrison, set out to write a book where he would tear down what he believed were 'primitive beliefs' about someone rising from the dead – and found himself writing *Who Moved the Stone?*, a book showing clearly that God did raise Jesus in bodily form.

Yes, Jesus did rise! He is alive now and for evermore! Praise God that both Old and New Testaments bear witness to this glorious fact.

What you can do during the coming week:
Get hold of a book which deals with the facts of the Resurrection. Read it yourself and pass it on.

STUDY 10

THE KING WHO IS COMING

QUESTIONS

DAY 1 *Psalm 110:1-2; John 18:33-37; Acts 2:34-36.*
a) What did *David* see the promised king doing?
b) How did Jesus indicate to Pilate that He was a king?

DAY 2 *Isaiah 9:6-7; 11:10; Micah 5:4-5a.*
a) What kind of king did *Isaiah* see in the future?
b) Why should we be particularly glad about Isaiah 11:10 (Rom. 15:10-12)?

DAY 3 *Jeremiah 23:5-6 (Good News Bible not accurate here); Zechariah 3:8.*
a) What term did *Jeremiah* use to describe the king he foretold (Isa. 11:1)?
b) What does this term suggest to you?
c) How can the knowledge that Jesus is 'The LORD Our Righteousness' help us today?

DAY 4 *Ezekiel 1:26-28; 34:22-24.*
a) How do we know that the figure *Ezekiel* saw in his vision was a king? Compare this with Revelation 4:2-3.
b) How do the verses in chapter 34 beautifully describe our Lord Jesus?

DAY 5 *Daniel 2:31-35, 44-45. (If you are not familiar with the story, read the whole chapter at home).*
a) What did *Daniel* see was the meaning of the stone in the king's dream?
b) 1 Peter 2:6-8. Peter quotes from Psalms and Isaiah to show us more about the Living Stone. What do you find out about Him here?

DAY 6 *Zechariah 9:9-10, 16; 14:3-9.*
a) Which parts of *Zechariah's* prophecy in chapter 9 have already come to pass, and which are still future?
b) Compare chapter 14:4 with Acts 1:11-12. What do you find?

QUESTIONS (contd.)

DAY 7 a) What have you learned in this study about Jesus when He comes again?

b) 2 Peter 3:1-14; Hebrews 10:25. What message is there here for us?

NOTES

In this study I see Jesus *as the great King who will one day reign supreme.*

* * *

It is fascinating to see how many of the prophecies about Jesus in the Old Testament have been fulfilled to the letter. As we read the Gospels, we see the whole life, death and resurrection of Jesus as the outworking of that which the prophets have written and dreamed about.

But this week we have stood beside prophets like Ezekiel and Zechariah, Daniel and Jeremiah, and looked over their shoulder to see what they say. And the difference here is that these events have not yet happened.

Does that mean they made a mistake?

We might think so, except for the fact that Jesus Himself, having fulfilled many of the Old Testament prophecies, was still looking forward to these particular ones. It is significant that the Second Coming of Christ is mentioned 318 times in the New Testament. If all the other prophecies we have been looking at have been fulfilled so exactly, is there any reason to suppose that these, about our King coming back, will not be?

The prophet Joel saw that in the days to come, God would pour out His Holy Spirit on all believers. We are living in those times. Joel prophesied that sons and daughters would prophesy and old men dream dreams. Let us pray for a clear vision of our Lord Jesus Christ as He will appear at the end of time. We need to see Him as the Mighty King, conqueror of evil, coming with all His angels to judge the world and to separate those who are clothed in His righteousness from those who are not.

If you belong to Him, you will thrill at the thought of that day when you will see Him face to face!

If you have not yet asked Him to forgive your sin and take control of your life there is still time, and you can make sure of your eternal destiny by accepting Him now.

A Prayer: 'Fill my eyes, O my God, with a vision of my Lord,
Fill my heart with love for Jesus, the coming King,
Fill my mouth with Thy praise,
Let me sing through endless days
"Take my will, let my life be wholly Thine."'

This week: Think carefully about the following advice –

Yes, my children, remain in union with him, so that when he appears we may be full of courage and need not hide in shame from him on the Day he comes (I John 2:28, GNB).

STUDY 11
SEEING JESUS IN OTHER PEOPLE

QUESTIONS

In this study we look at seven Old Testament characters, in whose lives we see a parallel to Jesus.

DAY 1 *Genesis 1:26-28; 1 Corinthians 15:21-22, 45-47.*
a) Before he sinned, in what ways was Adam like Christ?
b) What does Paul find (in Corinthians) by way of contrast, when he compares Adam with Christ?

DAY 2 *Genesis 14:17-20; Hebrews 7:1-3, 15-17.*
a) In what ways did Melchizedek foreshadow Christ?
b) Look back to *Study 5, Day 5.* What does it mean to us that Jesus is a priest?

DAY 3 In what ways was Joseph like Jesus? To find out, look up the following verses:

Genesis 37:3-4	(Luke 3:22)
Genesis 37:28	(Matthew 26:14-15)
Acts 7:9	(Philippians 2:7)
Genesis 39:7-10	(Hebrews 4:15)
Genesis 39:19-20	(Luke 22:54)
Genesis 41:39-43	(Philippians 2:9)
Genesis 42:6	(Philippians 2:10)

DAY 4 *Joshua 1:1-3*
a) What do you know about the story of Joshua? If possible, read it in a children's Bible Story Book.
b) Read Ephesians 2:4-10 and try to see how this is the spiritual counterpart of what Joshua did physically.

DAY 5 *1 Samuel 16:1-13.*
a) What parallels can you find between David and the Lord Jesus?
b) Can you think of some contemporary person whom God has chosen for a particular task?

QUESTIONS (contd.)

DAY 6 *I Kings 4:29-30; Matthew 12:42.*
a) What is the characteristic most usually associated with Solomon?
b) I Chronicles 22:6-10. What 4 things mentioned here about Solomon also apply to Jesus?

DAY 7 *Hosea 1:2-3; 3:1-2; I Peter 1:18-19.*
a) In what way was Hosea a type of Christ?
b) Summarise what you have seen of Jesus this week through the lives of these 7 characters.

NOTES

Different Old Testament characters *remind me of the Jesus I see in the New Testament.*

* * *

We have had a very brief look at some of the people who lived long before Christ. After He came, Christians did not say, 'My word, wasn't Jesus like Joshua in what He did? or Hosea?' No, they said, 'Now we can see that Joshua and Hosea and the others were types of the One who has now come into our midst.'
This was because:

1) Jesus was the most important person in history,
2) He was the perfect model, and though others were like Him, they were imperfect copies,
3) His whole life exemplified the things we have been thinking about, whereas Adam, Solomon, etc., reflected Him at just one particular stage of their lives.

Paul wrote:

'But we Christians ... can be mirrors that brightly reflect the glory of the Lord. And as the Spirit of the Lord works within us, we become more and more like him' (2 Cor. 3:18 LB).

Keep your eyes open to see people around you reflecting Jesus Christ in the next few weeks. It's thrilling to see Jesus in ordinary men and women who have been given that extraordinary touch by His Spirit.

* * *

Has this series of studies been 'a real eye-opener' to you? We have, indeed, seen Christ in the pages of the Old Testament and perhaps we shall have a greater appreciation of the One whom Moses and the prophets wrote about.

'Let the beauty of Jesus be seen in me,
All His wondrous compassion and purity,
O Thou Spirit Divine,
All my nature refine,
Till the beauty of Jesus be seen in me.'

T. M. Jones

ANSWER GUIDE

The following pages contain an Answer Guide. It is recommended that answers to the questions be attempted before turning to this guide. It is only a guide and the answers given should not be treated as exhaustive.

GUIDE TO INTRODUCTORY STUDY

Encourage free comment at the beginning, especially with newcomers, and remember that the 'right and wrong' may not be obvious to everyone.

After you have read what happened in Corinth, bring out the fact that Paul used the Old Testament to prove that Jesus was the Messiah. Show that Peter, Stephen and Philip also did this when talking to Jews (Acts 2:29-36; 7:52; 8:35).

Come prepared to teach the song (if possible!). Either get a friend to record it for you, or ask a guitar-playing member of your group to work on it, but do try to make it a theme for the whole series.

* * *

Take special note of the practical suggestions at the end of each week's notes. The Bible tell us not to 'merely listen to the word' but to 'do what it says', and you can encourage your group to apply the teaching in their own lives each week. You may like to share what you have done when you meet the following week.

Note:
Leaders, please note that God's mystery, hidden from all mankind in past ages, has been fully disclosed and revealed to all His people (Col. 1:25-28) once and for all in Jesus Christ. The gospel is still foolishness to those who do not believe (Matt. 11:25 and I Cor. 2:6-9). Its truth can only come to them by revelation from God.

GUIDE TO STUDY 1

DAY 1 a) We find that 'the Word', who later became a human being was the Agent of creation. Here is the first glimpse of God the Son.
b) 'We' indicates (as does the plural word 'Elohim' used here for God) more than one Person in the Godhead.

DAY 2 a) That He existed with God and as divine before the world was created, and gave up all that He had, to become man.
b) Personal.

DAY 3 a) Personal.
b) Personal.

DAY 4 a) 'The angel of the LORD.'
b) That they had seen God face to face.

DAY 5 a) He looked like a man, and it was only by what He said that Abraham knew that He was God.
b) Joshua threw himself on the ground in worship and offered himself to do whatever the Lord wanted.

DAY 6 a) In chapter 2, the 'angel' claims He was the one who led His people out of Egypt. In chapter 6 He promises to help Gideon do the impossible (v. 16).
b) He thought he was going to die (vv. 22-23).

DAY 7 a) He became flesh (or a human being),
God sent Him (His Son); He had a normal human birth; Jesus shared our human nature.
b) He was born of a human mother and lived and grew up as all people do; in the Old Testament He appeared as a fully grown man and disappeared.

GUIDE TO STUDY 2

DAY 1　a) He is the God of Abraham, Isaac and Jacob. He is the 'I AM'.
b) Because He claimed to be God by saying He existed before Abraham, and by using the term 'I AM' for Himself.

DAY 2　a) They were being cruelly treated as slaves in Egypt.
He would rescue them from the power of the Egyptians.
b) Jesus saves and ransoms those who trust in Him.

DAY 3　a) He said He was bread, He came down from heaven, He gives life, He satisfies.
b) Only by trusting in Him and then through meditating on Him.

DAY 4　a) The people had a need that could only be satisfied by one thing – water. God alone could satisfy that need. The water literally gave them life, they would otherwise have died.
b) Personal.

DAY 5　a) It had to be put on a pole, lifted up.
b) Look at it.
c) Be lifted up on a cross.
d) Believe in Him.

DAY 6　a) The Ark, and their obedience in doing what God said.
b) Believe in Jesus before the Judgment comes.
(Point out the similarity with Noah's day – no one believed that God would destroy the world.)

DAY 7　a) He saves us from being lost eternally, and sets us free from the fear of death.
b) Personal.

GUIDE TO STUDY 3

DAY 1   a) Jesus was God's only, beloved Son (v. 2), God went with Jesus to the place of sacrifice (v. 3), Jesus carried the cross (v. 6), God, His Father, willingly offered Him (v. 9).
b) The son, Isaac, was not actually killed; the ram died in his place (and so is an illustration of Jesus dying for us).

DAY 2   a) A one-year old male without any defects.
b) It would show that a substitute had already died in that home, so the eldest son would escape death.
c) He was our substitute, dying in our place.

DAY 3   a) Offer our bodies as a living sacrifice to God.
b) Personal. (You would need to explain the Levitical sacrifices, showing that they illustrate Christ voluntarily giving His life for us, and then explain that the sacrifice God requires of us is to live a life of self-denial and love to Him and others).

DAY 4   a) To take away sin and bring forgiveness.
b) Personal.

DAY 5   a) Sacrifice it and offer it as a sin offering.
b) He was to put his hands on its head, confess all the sins of the people over it and drive it away into the desert.
c) He carried our sins in His body on the cross.

DAY 6   a) As the life is in the blood, the animal had to die.
b) True forgiveness of sins and cleansing of our consciences (i.e. removal of guilt).

DAY 7   a) As a lamb, which seemed to have been killed.
b) The answer to this question is really all we have been studying this week.

GUIDE TO STUDY 4

DAY 1 a) Fine linen.
b) Either to keep something in or to keep the general public out.
That God (inside, as it were) was holy and perfect, and sinful man
could not come close to Him in just any old way.

DAY 2 a) White, blue, purple, red.
These colours may suggest different things to different people.
When they have shared, mention that in the Tabernacle, white was
for perfection (Christ's sinlessness), blue for the heavens (His
heavenly character), red for blood (His sacrifice), and purple, a
mixture of blue and red, and also the royal colour.
b) A gate is the way of entry. Jesus is the only way to approach the
Father.

DAY 3 a) It was the place where sacrifices were offered, pointing to His
supreme sacrifice.
b) The mirrors (shiny bronze) of the women who served at the
entrance to the Tent.
c) Cleansing from sin.

DAY 4 a) The table with the bread, the candlestick or lampstand, and the
golden altar of incense.
b) He came to be the Bread of Life, the Light of the world, and the
One who lives for ever to intercede for His people.

DAY 5 a) These Beings guarded the holiness of God against sinful man.
b) It was torn from top to bottom. God (from the top) has opened
up the way into His presence through the death of His Son.

DAY 6 a) Manna, Aaron's rod, the tables of stone.
b) Manna – Jesus is the bread from heaven.
Aaron's rod – Jesus is our great High Priest.
The tables of stone (the Law) – Jesus perfectly kept the Law.

DAY 7 a) That God is merciful and has provided a way for sinful man to be
forgiven.
b) He is the way.

GUIDE TO STUDY 5

DAY 1   a) To give him a message for the people.
b) He spoke to him face to face, clearly and not in riddles.

DAY 2   a) He would be like Moses, and from among the people of Israel.
b) He passed on to the people a message from God.
(Point out that a prophet was primarily a man who brought the word of God to his own people.)

DAY 3   a) Isaiah saw a vision of God and heard His call in the Temple.
Jeremiah heard God speaking to him.
Ezekiel saw a vision in the sky by the river and God spoke to him.
b) Each heard the word of God; each felt inadequate for the task of prophet; in each story God did something symbolical such as putting His words in their mouths.
If we feel inadequate to pass on God's word to others, we know that God can help us too.

DAY 4   a) They were amazed at the things He said and the authority with which He spoke.
b) 'The word of the LORD that came to ...'

DAY 5   a) They were the mediators between God and those who worshipped Him.
b) That He was the One by whom God would communicate to man, and man to God.

DAY 6   a) Both pleaded for their people (i.e. they were mediators).
b) He is our High Priest; He lives forever; He is holy, sinless, exalted; He offered one sacrifice, once and for all.

DAY 7   a) He knew of no-one to step in between God and him, and plead for him.
b) Jesus does just this.

FINDING CHRIST • ANSWER GUIDE . . . .

GUIDE TO STUDY 6

DAY 1
a) RSV: the Lord's Anointed; GNB: the king he chose; NIV: his Anointed One; LB: Messiah, Christ the king; NEB: his anointed king.
b) They conspire and plot against Him.
c) Herod, Pilate, Gentiles (Romans), and the people of Israel.

DAY 2
a) God has found, or chosen Him; God has anointed Him; God loves Him and makes Him victorious; He is God's firstborn son (2 Sam. 7: 8-14); the covenant with Him will be everlasting.
b) He will rule over the nations and His enemies will be crushed.

DAY 3
a) For the king of that day.
b) That God inspired this Psalm to be written to describe His Son.
c) He will love what is right and hate what is evil.

DAY 4
a) He acts in righteousness bringing salvation to His own people and judgment to His enemies.
b) The Redeemer must be righteous, so that He can pay the price; salvation is what He comes to bring; vengeance is meted out to those who do not repent and turn to Him.

DAY 5
a) Personal.
b) Personal.

DAY 6
a) An angel proclaimed Him as Christ at birth; the woman realised He was more than a human being; He performed miracles.
b) They said the Messiah would not come from Galilee, but from Bethlehem.

DAY 7
a) That He was the Messiah.
b) He didn't believe it.
c) Son of Man.

GUIDE TO STUDY 7

DAY 1   a) He was to be filled with God's Spirit, be gentle yet courageous and establish justice on the earth.
b) He was compassionate to those in need, yet courageous in the face of His enemies.
Many instances can be given, e.g. with the woman caught in adultery, but most notably at His trial.

DAY 2   a) The nation of Israel.
b) To restore God's people to greatness,
To be a light to the other nations.
c) Personal.

DAY 3   a) Jesus strengthened the weary; was beaten, insulted and spat upon; disfigured, despised and rejected; endured suffering and pain.
b) Rejection.

DAY 4   a) He would have told him about the arrest, trial and crucifixion of Jesus, and then gone on to tell about the Resurrection. He would then have explained to him the way of salvation.
b) Personal.

DAY 5   a) Verses 1, 6, 7, 8, 12, 13, 14, 15, 16, 17 and 18.
b) Tell them that because Jesus was forsaken by God on the cross when He took our sin, no one who trusts in Him will ever be forsaken by God. Jesus took that punishment instead of us.

DAY 6   One of His closest friends, who ate with him, betrayed Him (Luke 22:21).
He was alone on the cross and they gave Him vinegar (Luke 23:36).
He placed Himself into God's care (Luke 23:46).
Not one of His bones was broken (John 19:36).

DAY 7   a) Physical agony – all that He endured up to and on the cross.
Emotional agony – a friend betraying Him, others deserting Him, humiliation and insults.
These things all show that He was truly human.
b) Personal

GUIDE TO STUDY 8

DAY 1
a) He will crush the serpent's (devil's) head, 1 John 3:8.
b) He will come through Abraham, and all the nations of the earth will be blessed because of Him, Galatians 3:7-9.
c) The Promised One will come from the tribe of Judah, Hebrews 7:13-14.
d) A King, like a star, to come from Israel, Matthew 2:1-2; Revelation 22:16.

DAY 2
a) He will be born of a virgin, Luke 1:26-35.
b) He will come from Galilee, John 7:40-43.
c) He will be of the line of David, Matthew 1:6, 17.
d) He will be born in Bethlehem, Luke 2:1-6.

DAY 3
a) Kings will come to His birth, Matthew 2:9-11.
b) He will be called out of Egypt, Matthew 2:13-15.
c) God will send a forerunner, Mark 1:1-4.
d) The messenger will prepare the way, Matthew 11:7-10.

DAY 4
a) He will have a burning devotion to God's house of worship, John 2:13-17.
b) He will be a shepherd to His people, John 10:11.
c) He will be quiet and gentle, Luke 5:15-16.
d) He will ride into Jerusalem on a humble donkey, John 12:12-15.

NOTE:
Leaders, if your group has done all the questions at home, the answers can be given as above, otherwise you will need to take **DAYS 5, 6** and **7** separately.

GUIDE TO STUDY 9

DAY 1

a) The Resurrection, (I Cor. 15:17).

b) Peter on the day of Pentecost, and Paul in Antioch, both indicated that David died and was still dead, so the idea of resurrection was obviously pointing to someone else.

DAY 2

a) This undoubtedly refers to the heavenly kingdom, but can also be applied to Christians, who have already passed from death into life, and for whom physical death is simply a gateway into the Lord's presence.

b) Isaiah says that when Christ's life on earth is finished, He will 'see', 'be satisfied' and 'divide the spoils with the strong' – all things which a dead man cannot do.

DAY 3

a) He knows He will see God in his own (resurrection) body, and that when he does, his 'Redeemer' will be there (or 'the one who will come to his defence').
Personal.

b) They will have new, glorious bodies, which will be immortal, beautiful, strong and spiritual. We have this assurance because Christ was raised first.

DAY 4

Both worshipped God; were given a task by God – a mission to a rebellious people; both in a storm at sea; both presumed dead for 3 days; both raised to life again.

(An interesting point: 2 Kings 14:25 tells us that Jonah came from Gath Hepher. This town was only 3 miles away from Nazareth.)

Differences: Jonah disobeyed God and he did not actually die.

DAY 5

a) It would be written on their hearts by God, instead of in a book by Moses (Exod. 24:7).

(The whole Covenant of Exodus, chapters 20–23, was written in a book. Later, God wrote the 10 Commandments on stone – see Exodus 24:12 and 31:18.)

b) With blood.

c) The death and resurrection of the Lord Jesus.

DAY 6

a) As David their King.

b) To the time when the risen Jesus will reign as King.

DAY 7

a) That He was given authority, honour and kingly power over all the world; and that His Kingdom would last forever.

b) Personal.

GUIDE TO STUDY 10

DAY 1 a) Sitting in glory at the right hand of the Father, with all His enemies vanquished.
b) He spoke of 'My kingdom', and showed that although He was not an earthly king, He was King.

DAY 2 a) One wise, mighty, and ruling over an ever-growing peaceful kingdom. A descendant of David, drawing His strength from the Lord.
b) Because His eternal kingdom will be not only for the Jews, but also for Gentiles (including us).

DAY 3 a) A Branch.
b) Personal (e.g. a branch must come from an existing tree. New Bible Commentary: 'The fresh growth from the stump of a felled tree'.)
c) Because our own 'righteousness' falls far below God's standard, we would have no hope of coming to God if we did not take Christ as our righteousness (Rom. 4:6).

DAY 4 a) He was sitting on a throne.
b) They describe One who cares for His sheep and rules over them (Matt. 25:32-33)

DAY 5 a) He saw it as a kingdom that would never end and which would destroy all other empires.
b) The Living Stone is precious, placed by God as the cornerstone; He would be rejected, but would turn out to be the most important stone; some will stumble because of Him.

DAY 6 a) Past: the king has come riding on a donkey.
Future: verses 10 and 16.
b) Jesus ascended from the Mount of Olives and Zechariah prophecies that the Lord will stand there.

DAY 7 a) Personal.
b) As we wait for the day of the Lord, we should keep ourselves pure and free from sin, and encourage others to be ready too.

GUIDE TO STUDY 11

DAY 1   a) He was perfect, sinless, reflecting God's image. He had dominion over all the earth. In his 'kingdom' there was peace and prosperity.
b) Adam: brought death; in him, all die; human; from the earth. Christ: brought resurrection; in Him, all are made alive, spirit; from heaven.

DAY 2   a) He was: king of righteousness (Isa. 32:1); king of peace (Isa. 9:6); king and priest (both offices united only in Christ); like the Son of God (Heb. 7:3); lives forever – no beginning or end (most versions). (Some Commentators reject the view that Melchizedek was without ancestry or death, but we are taking Scripture at face value.)
b) He is the only one through whom we can approach God.

DAY 3   Joseph: beloved of his father; sold for money; became a slave; tempted, but without sin; arrested and condemned; exalted; worshipped.

DAY 4   a) Joshua was the leader who brought God's people into the Promised Land.
b) Just as the people of Israel wandered in the wilderness until Joshua brought them down into Jordan and then up into a new life, so we are brought into newness of life by Christ.

DAY 5   a) He was born in Bethlehem, was a shepherd, was God's chosen and anointed one who would later reign as king, the Holy Spirit controlled him.
b) Many examples will be given. Draw out the fact that all believers have been chosen by God, and He has a particular task for each one. It is our job to find out what it is (Rom. 8:29-30; 1 Cor. 12:4-6).

DAY 6   a) Wisdom. (If you have time you might like to compare human wisdom with wisdom from above, James 3:13-18. Also point to instances where Christ demonstrated His divine wisdom, e.g. Mark 12:17; John 8:7.)
b) He would rule in peace; His people would have peace and security; He would build the temple (Eph. 2:20-22); He would have a father/son relationship with God.

DAY 7 a) He brought back the wife who had been unfaithful and who had deserted him.

b) Jesus is sinless, brings life; is priest and king; suffered, then was exalted; leads His people to a new life; was chosen and anointed of God; is supreme wisdom; builds a spiritual Temple; is our Redeemer.

THE WORD WORLDWIDE

We first heard of WORD WORLDWIDE over 20 years ago when Marie Dinnen, its founder, shared excitedly about the wonderful way ministry to one needy woman had exploded to touch many lives. It was great to see the Word of God being made central in the lives of thousands of men and women, then to witness the life-changing results of them applying the Word to their circumstances. Over the years the vision for WORD WORLDWIDE has not dimmed in the hearts of those who are involved in this ministry. God is still at work through His Word and in today's self-seeking society, the Word is even more relevant to those who desire true meaning and purpose in life. WORD WORLDWIDE is a ministry of WEC International, an interdenominational missionary society, whose sole purpose is to see Christ known, loved and worshipped by all, particularly those who have yet to hear of His wonderful name. This ministry is a vital part of our work and we warmly recommend the WORD WORLDWIDE 'Geared for Growth' Bible studies to you. We know that as you study His Word you will be enriched in your personal walk with Christ. It is our hope that as you are blessed through these studies, you will find opportunities to help others discover a personal relationship with Jesus. As a mission we would encourage you to work with us to make Christ known to the ends of the earth.

Stewart and Jean Moulds – British Directors, **WEC International.**

A full list of over 50 'Geared for Growth' studies can be obtained from:
ENGLAND   John and Ann Edwards
5 Louvain Terrace, Hetton-le-Hole, Tyne & Wear, DH5 9PP
Tel. 0191 5262803 Email: rhysjohn.edwards@virgin.net

IRELAND   Steffney Preston
33 Harcourts Hill, Portadown, Craigavon, N. Ireland, BT62 3RE
Tel. 028 3833 7844 Email: sa.preston@talk21.com

SCOTLAND Margaret Halliday
10 Douglas Drive, Newton Mearns, Glasgow, G77 6HR
Tel. 0141 639 8695 Email: m.halliday@ntlworld.com

WALES   William and Eirian Edwards
Penlan Uchaf, Carmarthen Road, Kidwelly, Carms., SA17 5AF
Tel. 01554 890423 Email: Penlan.uchaf@farming.co.uk

UK CO-ORDINATOR
Anne Jenkins
2 Windermere Road, Carnforth, Lancs., LA5 9AR
Tel. 01524 734797 Email: anne@jenkins.abelgratis.com

UK Website: www.wordworldwide.org.uk

Christian Focus Publications

publishes books for all ages

Our mission statement –

STAYING FAITHFUL

In dependence upon God we seek to help make His infallible word, the Bible, relevant. Our aim is to ensure that the Lord Jesus Christ is presented as the only hope to obtain forgiveness of sin, live a useful life and look forward to heaven with Him.

REACHING OUT

Christ's last command requires us to reach out to our world with His gospel. We seek to help fulfill that by publishing books that point people towards Jesus and help them to develop a Christ-like maturity. We aim to equip all levels of readers for life, work, ministry and mission.

Books in our adult range are published in three imprints.

Christian Focus contains popular works including biographies, commentaries, basic doctrine, and Christian living. Our children's books are also published in this imprint.

Mentor focuses on books written at a level suitable for Bible College and seminary students, pastors, and other serious readers. The imprint includes commentaries, doctrinal studies, examination of current issues, and church history.

Christian Heritage contains classic writings from the past.

For details of our titles visit us on our website
www.christianfocus.com

ISBN 0 908067 39 9

Copyright © WEC International

Published in 2002 by
Christian Focus Publications, Geanies House,
Fearn, Ross-shire, IV20 ITW, Scotland
and
WEC International, Bulstrode, Oxford Road,
Gerrards Cross, Bucks, SL9 8SZ

Cover design by Alister MacInnes

Printed and bound by J.W. Arrowsmith, Bristol

Unless otherwise stated, quotations from the Bible are from the New International Version, © 1973, 1978, 1984 by International Bible Society, published in Great Britain by Hodder and Stoughton Ltd.